LEARNING TO MAKE AN OUD
IN NAZARETH

LEARNING TO MAKE AN OUD IN NAZARETH

Ruth Padel

Chatto & Windus
LONDON

Published by Chatto & Windus

4 6 8 10 9 7 5 3

First published in Great Britain in 2014 by
Chatto & Windus
Random House, 20 Vauxhall Bridge Road,
London SW1V 2SA
www.randomhouse.co.uk

Addresses for companies within The Random House Group Limited can be found at:
www.randomhouse.co.uk/offices.htm

The Random House Group Limited Reg. No. 954009

A CIP catalogue record for this book
is available from the British Library

ISBN 9780701188160

Penguin Random House is committed to a sustainable future for
our business, our readers and our planet. This book is made from
Forest Stewardship Council® certified paper.

Printed and bound in Great Britain by Clays Ltd, St Ives plc

Set in Minion 11/14 pt
Typeset by Palimpsest Book Production Limited, Falkirk, Stirlingshire

For Nikos Stavroulakis and Etz Hayyim Synagogue, Hania
for the Trio Joubran from Nazareth
and for Graham and Peggy Reid who introduced me to their music

In his hands he held the clear-voiced lyre
wondering whether to seek asylum
at the courtyard altar
or run forward and beg for his life.
He placed his lyre on the ground
between the mixing-bowl and silver chair . . .

HOMER, *The Odyssey*
Book 22, Slaughter of the Suitors

Contents

Learning to Make an Oud in Nazareth

The first day he cut rosewood for the back,
bent sycamore into ribs and made a belly
   of mahogany. *Let us go early to the vineyards*
   and see if the vines have budded.
The sky was blue over the Jezreel valley
   and the gilt dove shone
above the Church of the Annunciation.
The second day, he carved a camel-bone base
   for the fingerboard.
I sat down under his shadow with delight.

The third day he made a nut of sandalwood,
and a pick-guard of black cherry.
   He damascened a rose of horn
   with arabesques
as lustrous as under-leaves of olive beside the sea.
   I have found him whom my soul loves.
He inlaid the sound-hole with ivory swans,
each pair a valentine of entangled necks,
   and fitted tuning pegs of apricot
to give a good smell when rubbed.

The fourth was a day for cutting
high strings of camel-gut. *His left hand*
   shall be under my head.
   For the lower course, he twisted copper
pale as tarmac under frost.
   He shall lie all night between my breasts.
The fifth day he laid down varnish.

Our couch is green and the beams of our house
    are cedar and pine. Behind the neck
he put a sign to keep off the Evil Eye.

My beloved is a cluster of camphire
in the vineyards of Engedi
    and I watched him whittle an eagle-feather, a plectrum
    to celebrate the angel of improvisation
    who dwells in clefts on the Nazareth ridge
where love waits. And grows, if you give it time.
Set me as a seal upon your heart.
On the sixth day the soldiers came
    for his genetic code.
We have no record of what happened.

I was queuing at the checkpoint to Galilee.
I sought him and found him not.
    He'd have been in his open-air workshop –
    I called but he gave me no answer –
the self-same spot
    where Jesus stood when He came from Capernaum
to teach in synagogue, and townsfolk tried
to throw Him from the rocks. Until the day break
    and shadows flee away
I will get me to the mountain of myrrh.

The seventh day we set his wounded hands
around the splinters. Come with me from Lebanon,
    my spouse, look from the top
    of Shenir and Hermon, from the lions' dens.

On the eighth there were no more days.
I took a class in carpentry and put away the bridal rug.
We started over
with a child's oud bought on eBay.
   He was a virtuoso of the oud
and his banner over me was love.

The Wanderer

I met him at dusk in the courtyard where they weave the tents
for Sukkot, a wanderer who had come into his own.
The olive tree had been hard-pruned along its central branch
and only the tips were in leaf, grey fingers stretching to light,
but you could see new growth, a haze of turquoise rust.
Roots blistered the sea-pebble paving to a mound
and I thought of the black ceramic bird my mother notched
in the centre of her pies, whose yellow beak cracked the crust.

He had a cello in his hand. The grain glowed peat-swirl
brown of a mountain tarn, maroon under the f-holes
as if someone had been at it with mammoth blood.
The spike glittered between two stones. Take this,
he said. I'm giving it to you. I looked away
at marble grooves framing the half-dome niche
where a tap hangs over a copper cup chained to the wall
then ran my finger down the neck and scroll.

I imagined lifting the broken handle of the amphora
stuck face-down under the tree like history keeping a lid
on rising roots. The past is not where you left it. Every choice
is loss. That corridor you didn't follow, the gate
to unknown woods, the unexplored stair, the blue door
you never found time to open – they whirl within
cracking the floor. I met him at twilight where they put up
the tent for Sukkot: a wanderer who had come into her own.

The Electrification of Beth Shalom

I am looking too hard, or this scene is looking too hard
at me. Turn of the century and the last Chief Rabbi of Crete
is standing by seven naked bulbs, the first electric light
in town. What of the chandelier, a shiver of gold
chrysanthemums – or, if you prefer, the roof?
He has decades to go, this Rabbi. They'll bury him in 1933.

But eight years on, avalanches of black fire
pouring from Luftwaffe bombers, rumble and rubble,
thunder flash like the crack of doom
and the whole island a furnace, lit
and ravaged by the *simurgh*, behemoth or *ziz* –
who could have foreseen that? This is prayer

sung for the first time in bright light, a dreaming
into chinks between old stones gleaming
edge to edge. Chain, bevel, flex and switch
and no way out, no way at all for between-thinking
as the glare disappears and then the walls themselves
like a drop laid on the tongue. *Listen*, says the dark.

Landscape with Flight into Egypt

Here we are in mountains at a pass
between two shadows before we descend
the black path. Against a blue inlet
fretted with tow-coloured towns, a tall pine

falls to an upside-down cross. An idol
slips out of a shrine. Over the gulf, a crow
squats on a leafless stump. Landscape
is your life seen in distance, when you know

for just an interval of sunlight
how to join time travelled with time still to go.
We have passed a red scatter of anemones
with no fore-memory of blood. In front and behind

are cities, all that sweet clustering of *civilised*.
In one, the massacre we're running from.
The other is asylum. I can't see your eyes
and you can't see mine but a white bird flies

across the shadowed precipice, and the ravine
we have to go down into. It's us and the child.
Home is the journey. Home is the wild
with no one to share it, no one to stand and gaze

at pale light falling on arches, alley-ways
and ziggurats clenched in their own lives
like crowds dancing in the street outside
while the Lover, the Singer, dies.

The Hebrew for Egypt Means Narrow

This iron lamp burning on the courtyard wall
at Passover is a cage of wasted light in daytime.
Someone has forgotten or not noticed
and the wise child would turn it off.

But I don't, I sit under it after spring rain
in this garden of chipped
inscriptions and new-risen sap
beside white pebbles placed on broken slabs

for rabbis buried when citizens here
were too hostile to chance a trip
to the burying ground at the edge of town.

We are out in the wilderness now. Behind
is the word for Egypt. Narrow, constrained –
but an easy life. Do you want to go back?

Extract from the Travels of Ibn Jubayr

How we need each other, crossing this desert
of life, says the Master returned to Granada
from the Haj. The last water we found
was an uncased well. Sand had fallen in.
The camel-leader sought to dig the water out
but failed. Next day we entered 'Aydhab.
We waited in air so hot it melts the flesh
with nothing to eat save what we'd brought.
Ships came and went from India and the Yemen.
Citizens there live off the pilgrims
who carry their own food in, pay a daily tax
and wait for the *jilab* to Jeddah.
You buy a one-way ticket in advance,
sit in the open boat like chickens in a coop

and cross a drift-born desert, a mountain range
of fog and snow, then the clash and whistling of more sea
with your soft palate open like chalk. You can't help it,
you're in hands of the living God. You come to a border
patrolled by laws you'll never know. You hardly talk.
Your mouth is dry. These are the crossings of faith:
you go where daemon blows.
Winds carry you to anchorage, a land
where tall, silent, mountain Sudanese
mount you on camels and lead you through mirages,
through days and nights of sand. They seize
everything if you perish. Those who survive
come in like men throwing off a shroud
and lie down under flowering trees.

The Chain

Why do I keep thinking about that chain?
I didn't dream it up, I wasn't born
when Moshe Scheiner made it. But yes
if I'd had the skill . . . Torn out of my life
I guess if I found a broom-handle
broken from its head, I'd recognise
something I could turn, with a knife,
to linked medallions. I'd start picturing a cartouche –
no, four or five – between a run of loops.
When does chain connect and when does it spell
prison, manacle, a cry for help, regalia of office?
I'd be, at least, a witness.

Casting chains for the ships of Solomon.

On the first lunette, where the handle snapped
from the worn-out bristles, I'd show us saying goodbye.
Though that was not the word they used –
they spoke French or maybe Polish, and the baby
didn't speak at all. I'd carve myself, a father with his son:
he's hugging my knees while I dandle the little one.
That's where I'd begin, scraping where sap
once rose in a pine-wood heart, aiming not for the under-
image of intaglio but for raised relief: an upper layer,
an outline to tell the world what happened here.
A sequence of, as it were, wood-gems in umber.
Engraved and polished like cameos in carnelian.

Wreaths of chain to ornament the temple.

For the links, I'd try out diagrams in the dust.
Sketching, half-remembering different kinds
of tensile loop – jump ring, pig-holder,
torus, daisy, curb – till I hit on a design like a safety-pin
without the springing free. Copying what swivels do
with studs to prevent tangle, I'd mimic the effect
of a metalworker pulling wire through smaller
and smaller dies, then winding it round a mandrel.
I'd imagine him, my ghost-glass alter ego,
keeping pace with me through the night
in the tiny brilliance of one candle. Cutting,
bending each link closed, then dripping in the solder.

Why stand far off, O Lord? Why hide Thyself in times of trouble?

On the next cartouche, I'd carve myself
walking away from the perimeter fence
at Beaune-la-Rolande. It's only half-built, but I know
the Madsen guns are lining up behind.
I'm alone, lugging timber into that damnable hut
as to a tomb. To represent, to withdraw in your mind,
is not escape. You can't say I've side-stepped reality.
On the third, I'm pushing a loaded barrow
with an armed guard to supervise. For the fourth, no
people: only the low-roofed bunkers, black inside.
On the last, wives and children wave goodbye
to men boarding a train. One day, that will be me.

Shall Thy wonders be known in the dark?

I'd keep the penknife hidden. Brushing ice
from the inner window-pane on winter nights
I'd carve the end into the bearded head
of a patriarch or rabbi. Each of his hairs
takes weeks. Like prayers at Rosh Hashanah
I'm trying to transform sin into grace. A snail
can't crawl on the straight razor and live.
You'd laugh to see the stages, how odd it looked
half-done: a chain sliding out of a stick, a grey pole
alchemising halfway down to honey rings
like dunged straw into gold. And the new work sweet
as a book you treasure but haven't yet cut the pages.

I cry in the day but Thou hearest not, and in the night season.

I'd work along the spindle never knowing
if the links are really there. I'm lost in the river.
Strong bulls of Bashan have encircled me.
Gouging a negative, searching for air
within one wooden oval to begin the next
inside, so they'll shift against each other,
sets me free. But outside or in, still the old question –
is this discovery or true making? Are the forms
of shaping mine? *I will wake the dawn.*
I will toss my sandal on Edom. Blur your eyes
and it's the paper chain my children made
to decorate the hearth. *Will You be angry for ever?*

After the Fire

for Etz Hayyim, after arson

If you sit and look through a repeating sheaf
of open doors – double folds to the west
where the Sabbath bride enters at sundown

double folds to the east where the ghosts gather
asking us to listen, please listen and remember;
if you carry on looking, taking in

the twisted ring-handles, brass locks and demi-lunars
of stained pine fitted to the frame
of each white ancient arch – you'll see a strip of green:

the Y of a pomegranate tree, lobes
of young fern, flesh spears of an iris leaf
and the soft blue stem of a Persian rose.

A Guide to the Church of Nativity in Time of Siege

Come in *seigneur*. Quick. Let me show you round.
Bend please, the gate is four-foot-three. We call it
Door of Humility. You can interpret this in many ways.
God He is found by many paths. Some say
this little entry speaks today of hope.
Write in your paper, if you like, this gate reminds
of other trouble times our church survived.
So, take your breath. You're safe now, friend.
Touch the inside wall – you have at your fingers' end
the start of the Church herself. This basilica you see
was built by Emperor Justinian, sixth century AD.
But underneath is earlier. The past is not lost
but covered up by time. Beneath us is first
church of all: basilica of Constantine,
founded two hundred years before, on living rock,
to Mary *Theotokos*. In English, *Giving Birth*.
Not the Madonna with her Child, although
her lily is our native flower. You're free sir,
you can go to lime-sinks of the north
and find it blooming now. Here, in the nave,
I lift a hatch. See the lower floor
like snakeskin – amber, black and gold
key-pattern geometry, in parallel?
Roman mosaic, laid in 324.
Last week mortar shells from tanks outside
smashed many *tesselles* – in English, *tesserae* –
but many survive unbroken. Seventeen
hundred years – and our church rests
on these. Above, she's fortified. Like a castle? True.
Asylum is *safe place* but Emperor Justinian knew

make safe must be *defend*. He built high walls
round Bethlehem so church might stay wide open
with triple arch – three doors – for visitors like you.
In Ottoman times, these wide doors were blocked
so Turkish *giaours* could not gallop in on war-stallions.

Did you bring water? Medicine? Food?
Well – what we have provide, must do.
Come into the shadows, among rows
of ginger pillars made for Constantine.
Strange colour, no? A forest of pink and brown.
Run your finger down warm sandstone, quarried
from local hills – where you may see
the Holy Bible's orchards. Pomegranate
blossom, scarlet in green leaves.
Wild almond. Purple cream of Judas trees:
in flower now, spring season, when he hung himself.
See the flicker when I move the door a crack?
A shimmer like spider silk on Corinth-petal
capitals, every pillar? Have you seen flakes
of mother-of-pearl on column heads before?
Our town is famous, sir, for mother-of-pearl.
We understand vulnerability. How to carve
spirals, pentangles and curls
without a break. Other time, if you like,
you can see my brother's shop for gifts.
He sells drop-earrings like milk air,
colliers translucides, and buttons cut
as roses, birds and fish. Sorry, no spare
candle: take my hand down stairs to crypt

where Nativity took place. In the Bible
it is stable. Here, a cave. In AD 135
Roman Emperor Hadrian proclaimed
this cave was sacred to a pagan god, Adonis.
He made it criminal, for Christians to say God
was born in here. But even emperors bow to time.
After two hundred years, Helena put her hand
into this rock. She found a basin made of mud
and clay. The Manger. Touch, sir. It is allowed.
Her son, first Christian Emperor Constantine,
built his basilica above. They were not proud:
they were late-comers to our faith.
In the Bible, never too late to remake
who you are. In the next cave, Saint Jerome
translated the Holy Bible into Latin. Next cave,
these mounds in the dark are babies' graves.
King Herod told his soldiers to exterminate
the little sons of Bethlehem. Did you see
Schindler's List? Remember the lone horseman
on a hill above the ghetto, watching soldiers bayonet
house-doors, drag children out of wardrobes,
out from under beds? That happened here also –
in Manger Square, where you came in. The Massacre
of Innocents. All mothers of Bethlehem
screaming for their sons. But nothing is as it was.
The crib is covered up in silver. Justinian
spread marble over cave walls and roof, and floor.

You like this gold fringe round the manger?
The inner veil, blue silk like cupola of heaven

with white lace angels, came from the Isle of Cos.
On the floor, Greek priests inlaid a silver star
to mark the spot where His feet first touched ground.
Fourteen points, like fourteen wavy flames,
and fourteen silver lamps above, to represent
communities over the world who worship here.
The floor-marble is stained where screws have let in rain
but our church is sustained by every heart upon the planet.
That's why you've come sir, isn't it? Everyone dreams
of celebrating liturgy or Pentecostal Feast
at these two altars, face to face across the cave.
Altar of the Manger and – turn please –
the Magi. You're standing, friend,
where Wise Men from the East
stood – knelt, I should say – with offerings.

Have you seen Shepherds' Field outside our town?
That's where the sky lit up. Christmas cards
in other countries show this scene
with holly, deer and snow. But it happened here
with olive-tree trunks shining in angel-glow
and our flowers – Palestine White Iris, Bethlehem
Milk Vetch – sleeping in winter ground.
Our shop sells olive-wood figures, beautiful.
Three different kings, a donkey, ox and camel;
sheep and their shepherds playing bagpipes;
a shepherd boy with a lamb about his neck
running to tell about the angel.

Our basilica is heart of Bethlehem. Convents cling
and cluster to its walls like snow-drop bulbs.

They say that from the air we look like ivory
carved from a single tusk. But our town must be
most captured, most destroyed, in history.
In 614, Persian armies broke down the city walls
and many houses. But they saw Byzantine
mosaics, they recognised the holiness
of Wise Men's clothes – and left the church alone.
Everyone finds what's sacred to them here.
In 634, Arabs captured Bethlehem
and made a Muslim shrine in the basilica.
In 747, Bethlehem fell again – this time
in earthquake. The Holy Land is rifted, sir.
We stand on clashing wounds beneath earth's crust.
Yet the same thing happened, even in the act of God –
town crumbled to dust but church OK.
In eleventh century, Crusades coming from West,
was anger against Christians here, but Al-Hakim
didn't danger church because of Muslim shrine.
Everything played its part. Then, siege of Jerusalem.
Tancred the Norman took the town in 1099.
On Christmas Day 1101, Baldwin was crowned
first High Crusader King of Outremer.
But history is a revolving door. Nothing here
lasts long that's from outside. In Arabic and Hebrew
verb *to be* does not exist. No Present, only Future
and the Past. The Crusader kingdom fell
1187 . . . Am I boring you?
Every time till now our white small town
was crush to powder-stone, the church survived.
That's all I meant to say. Everyone let it be.
Never siege before. Yet it looked in 1350

17

as you see now – a citadel. All the West
gave money to protect. Philip of Burgundy
sent pinewood. Edward IV sent roof lead
packed in straw from English fields. Just so
America is sending help, you'll see. America
is Christian land. They believe – and we, we need.
We are taking care of hundreds here. Children,
mothers, novices and priests. Ill, hungry, dying –
and bodies of the dead, decomposing in most holy site
of Christendom. And most holy time, at Easter . . .
You are leaving, sir? I thought you were a friend.
If you think my speech is wrong,
I'm not myself today. I would have taken you to the garden,
shown you flowers of the Bible, that belongs
to everyone. Blue alkanet, white asphodel . . .
This is your story, too. What happens to the man
who has betrayed or – well – pretends?
Bend please. The door is four-foot-three.
If you return, it may be all you see
is tinsel among rubble, heaven rolled back
like mourning cloth on a market stall
as if the Child we honour were stillborn,
and all the darnels of the Bible. Spiny zilla,
Syrian acanthus, grey nightshade, Christ Thorn.

Seven Words and an Earthquake

I *Forgiveness*

Olives in blue-tissue mist. Sunrise in the *wadi*
one Friday in spring. Bare creviced hills
pink-threaded with cyclamen and flax,

wild almond in bloom and leaves of the rock
rose, green on grey stone. Three gazelles
on the ridge, running. But you, you're on your back

facing sky like mother-of-pearl, in a body
you can't climb out of.
If you could turn your head, you'd see dry

stalks of last winter's grass
lit by rays you feel you could touch:
rays like ingots of fluff,

spokes of a broken wheel, almost
horizontal, piercing the halo of dust
round visitors coming up the path from town.

Alone last night at full moon, you prayed so hard
your sweat was blood. Capillaries broke like straw
and leaked into your pores. Handcuffed

you found others to care about. The guard
who whacked you in the mouth
for keeping silent under questioning; squaddies

expert in the flay, who sliced skin off your back
and shoulders; the centurian with digital timer
who posed by your naked body. Anything goes

at the checkpoint, the cell, the interview-room.
Untied, you slumped to flagstones
purple as Judas blossom with your blood.

A laughing soldier wove barbed strands
of caperbush – in Hebrew *avionah*,
also called Desire, whose white buds

freckle the slopes at Capernaum like talc –
into a crown of claws and pushed it through
the vascular fretwork of your scalp.

But now you're with the experts. They do this week in
week out: jam someone's naked spine
and scapula, oozing sheafs

of opened muscle, against rough timber,
like this lumber you've dragged through the city.
They tie your arms to the T-beam

allowing for flexion. *Largo, largo* –
they've been told to ratchet up the pain.
You can't hope for the easy option, nails

in the hollow below the wrist, the Only-Use-Metal way
of making sure the hands won't shred
and the whole boiling

cascade off the cross. No, with rope to take your weight
the man with mallet and spike can safely penetrate
the star-centre of your palm where life-curve

crosses line of the heart and the ulnar nerve
begins its delicate run. Each arm, through brachial
plexus, root-nerve, nape

and on up the back of your skull
will feel on fire for the duration, the who-knows-how-
many hours this Friday business will take.

There's more where that came from, the whole human brew
of jealousy and spite. So you displace. You think of the others.
Father forgive them for they know not what they do.

II *Comfort*

Soft-leaved *batha. Garrigue* in full blaze of morning.
They pull down your feet
keeping the knees flexed, press left
over right and hammer a ten-inch pin
through the arch of both. Bluebottles glint
on the mingled blood as when a village woman
stretches thread outside her house, weft
and warp between pegs in the dust, and children
marvel at green and pink together. They love
the shot-silk blend growing as she weaves
andante, with a gentle *click-thud*.

Yes, think of that as the eyes drink you in,
greedy to see what you'll do, arms out like wings
as they winch you up in brightening sun.
Beyond the faces, familiar desert-scrub
and shadow of the sparrowhawk.
Torn blossom floats towards earth, over the lime-
stone footprint of a dinosaur, which must have tramped
through cooling flow to those indigo hills –
where the gold gill of daylight swam up
hours ago now, in a tender lemony glow –
and over the weeping olive trees of Palestine.

Pedlars sell souvenirs. Citron peel
litters the ground. Up here, a dripping sound.
Whimper-sobs like a run-over dog. Hours crawl by
like a serpent mortally wounded. Soldiers toss dice

in the dirt. *We are paying,* the blue air whispers,
for what we did wrong. Someone curses in Aramaic.
Furies rise from black earth. *Remember me when you come
into your kingdom.* With a hanging head
it's a struggle to even inhale, let alone speak,
but again you think of the other. That's the deal.
Tonight, I promise, you'll be with me in Paradise.

III *Relationship*

That time he was sleepy as the moon
   and she carried him three hours to the priest.

The chip of kingfisher lapis she tied round his wrist
   to turn away the evil eye – where did that go?

He was shy in the playground.
   Afraid of heights

of fire at night. Yesterdays glisten
   like photos melting together in the rain.

Prints of small feet in wet sand.
   His first step without holding her hand.

Keeping him quiet in siesta, mending clothes
   through those long mother-afternoons

you think will never end. The first glint of a tooth,
   first pair of shoes. Whose days were those? Blink

and they're gone. Is he most her son
   not back then but now, when he disowns her

and gives her to his friend? She used to listen
   as if everything he said was truth,

would turn to gold. But these words come to her
   like rubble at ends of the earth. Does he think

24

he's looking after her? She's been dismissed.
   He's done, it seems, with relationship. Like a lover

breaking a bond. As if bond did not exist.
   Woman, behold thy son. Son, behold thy mother.

IV *Abandonment*

What breeds about the smoke-house of the heart?
This is it now, the central ceremony
of let's-not-look-away from the great stone ring
of you on your own, under a rug of flies.

The bubble-wrap of viscid spittle down your chin
has dried like gluey fire consumed by its own ash.
New agony begins: crushing pain in the deep chest.
The fortress membrane – built like the wall of China

as a double palisade, to keep in roots of the aorta,
vena cava, pulmonary vein and this *shump-shump*
of muscle pushing blood through shattered cells –
is silting up with serum and starts to compress the heart.

Eclipse. Where's healing now? You've lived
for others' feelings. You've seen darkness over earth,
the forked stick on the path. Now it's mucus on the lip,
mouths of wounds peeling to black. You long to melt to air

but you've no choice, except the ancient tongue
called vulnerability. This was it, your one shot at experience:
circumference of human skin, swirling bitumen of self.
This is the ocean floor of all you've been –

that you're alone with pain, that's what you're for.
No angels around now to make wise men go home
by another route, avoiding the jealous king
who persecutes; who says *OK, destroy your own.*

Untouchable means separate. *Where have you taken me?*
You trusted to a lifelong call. Mistakenly.
It must have been echo, or projection.
Watch the double walls of the pericardium

slip against each other like wet leaves
and overflow with serum. Shout in a loud voice
and the new, metallic-tasting dark translates.
My God why have you forsaken me?

V *Need*

The sticking point is how to ask for help:
that black hole
of showing you have need. One verb stands

for every thread of bruise-broke-opens,
the scarlet web of toxins round the body
like acres of shucked plastic choking up the sea.

What you're most afraid of: leaving it to others –
giving up control, having to beg
not even for compassion but the *pizzicato* drops

and pure dream stream of water – because you might be mocked
and disappointed. So you will. Cohorts of the night,
the envious and vengeful, the *Schadenfreude* guys

are ready with the evil eye, their own sour wine
and the sponge at the end of a spear. Curved shields
of the Occupiers rock empty on the earth.

They're here and they're not allowed to leave
until this body's dead. It's growing dark.
Partridges scuttle from the path. A beak of sky

tears desiccating innards. Cells collapse
like a high-rise after bomb blast, a bonfire
of wattle and daub. Your own weight is choking you.

Like a gazelle garrotted by razor-wire
every breath bites deeper into flesh, every tug
pulls the metal closer. The dream is gone

of being looked after. You're a planet without orbit
in heaven black with silt. Some membrane
between asylum and massacre has burst.

It's almost over. Ratchet of the heart
valve splitting. The flame almost blown out
in a storm lantern that lit the universe

for other people. Still you cannot ask
direct. The wrecked lungs grasp
at hyphenettes of oxygen. The heart, submersed,

struggles to shift sluggish thickening red cells
but the dehydrated tissues won't stop sending
stimuli to the brain till you gasp it out. *I thirst.*

VI *Fulfilment*

Antlers of sacrifice. Air like black chiffon. Chill
creeping through decaying veins. *Lento, lento*:
a smell of burning rubber,
static on an ambisonic microphone
and a spine, a bone zip, trying to keep together
what's falling apart: at three in the afternoon,
the hour children are let out of school to go home.
We're all here in our own sequences, the body
in sepsis and collapse. But a white bird comes
like quartz through coal-dark sky,
a needle of light cutting the scene in half
to say you're not alone
                                            everything that separates
unites, and yes there was point to all the mire
and godforsakenness. It wasn't just illusion,
shedding the mantle of self, hanging in when the going
gets tough. The rainbow's end is your own slice
of *good enough*. The story, the gash in time
begun with an outcast birth, is never sealed
but you have to feel it all. You can't do *numb.*
Fire-bolts of steel through your palms. Tissues tear
in your back when you shift down splintery timber.
No morphine to tip in your throat but you're nearly
there and you whisper, *Done. It's done.*

VII *Reunion*

Who are the guilty? One more breath enters the lungs.
This is neither silence nor speech but a cross-roads,
a sunset at dawn. Asphyxia, head on the chest,
the far point of powerlessness

in eyes of a blinded robin. The throb of yellow
jelly in the heart has nearly stopped. What will it be
to join the Other who you know is here with you?
Can you give up your soul? Something is slipping free

like the repeated nonsense syllable
that turned out to be you learning to talk.
Packets of memory jag before your eyes.
Holding her hand to name the planets

and gazing at noctilucent cumulus,
flame, maroon and white
like the bolt of zig-zag silk from Samarkand
she found to wrap you in. The crowd below

buzzing like filaments of a clapped-out electric heater
could be humming lullabies to fauna of the night:
the shy Arabian leopard and golden spiny mouse
of Palestine. Go where it hurts most. In a last surge

of strength, press the severed metatarsal bone
against the nail. Straighten your knees, inhale
a last deep breath. You're one minute from home.
Father, into your hands I commit my spirit.

Afterword

The voices of self are over. A sepia
penumbra clears round a moon of blood.

The ancient temple cloth, sixty feet high,
four inches thick – twisted scarlet,

blue and purple thread protecting other people
from the sacred –

tears in two. Earth trembles and will not stop.
Feldspar, formed on the abyssal plain

of the ocean floor, splits *presto*
and goes on splitting. Rocks crack

like cannon-fire and the East Nazareth
mountains echo in aftershock

over limestone braille
of the Dead Sea Rift or Fault

over aquifers, flint and fissured chalk
and barbed wire on the Mount of Olives.

Violence. Take your finger off the edge
and it snaps back like a rubber band.

Buckling. Compression. A spear jabs
through an interspace between the ribs

and water gushes out with blood from the fluid sac.
This is the end of everything you've been.

God is what God does. You are the earth.
The outer world, body's integument, layers

of all that's happened in a life,
bastions of defence and muddled litter

of experience, are bleeding out like dye
into a shroud. We are rhythmic

animals and our prayer is breath.
We don't need *veil*.

The mystery we call soul
is no password-protected secret

but an invitation. You'll get there.
You've come home

to new possibilities of you. The night glides by.
Clouds move fast and free across the sky.

As I Flick the Remote in the Gulf I Think of an Ancient Greek Playwright

At home the same things happened. Women
were widowed and died. Parents shuffle
through empty rooms without the sons they loved.
It was our troops. They did this in our name.
We hold our tongue about such acts of shame.

Euripides, with your scalpel pity and your songs,
who watched from exile in Macedonia
that nation where you spoke out against massacre
(blowing up allies, for God's sake)
sizzle in its turn, and the city walls pulled down:

you who were torn to pieces on a goat-track
by dogs – what's the use? I think of you walking
in oak-forests of the north, where racing mares
graze meadows which Athenian yeomen,
blunting their hoes on rock, would kill to cultivate.

You're imagining, as you hike, a new god,
baby-faced with Elvis sideburns, ivy sap
running down his microtonal oud,
entering every city: twin-towered. barbarian, Greek.
But this is March 2006. I'm on the edge of a bed

watching CNN through cappuccino shades of afternoon
in the freezing cold Mövenpick Hotel, Bahrain.
100 degrees outside and the manager can't turn off
the air conditioning. No one can. Cement roofs roil
up and down, far as the eye can see:

34

an eyeful of caramel domes and salmon sky
in the first Gulf State to find oil.
I'm watching the President of Iran
in ivory denim conduct a dance
of seven ministers. They hop in celebration.

Old men like a tragic chorus, round and round
a desk of microphones like the crown of hills
about a holy city. They have enriched plutonium.
Do they feel a touch ridiculous, too? Representatives
of other Arab states, my friends downstairs, are calm.

No big deal, no cause for alarm. But Washington
is talking of war. Euripides, whose microtones
I lived with a long strange while,
where are your arguments now: that frayed silk rope
of human, divine and the same rules applying to all?

The Just-World Hypothesis

JEREMY PAXMAN: *Does the fact that George Bush and you are Christians make it easier for you to view these conflicts in terms of good and evil?*

TONY BLAIR: *I think whether you're a Christian or not you can try to perceive what is good and what is evil.*

JEREMY PAXMAN: *You don't pray together, for example?*

TONY BLAIR: *No we don't pray together Jeremy, no.*

JEREMY PAXMAN: *Why do you smile?*

TONY BLAIR: *Because – why do you ask me the question?*

JEREMY PAXMAN: *Because I'm trying to find out how you feel about it.*

TONY BLAIR: *Possibly.*

— Transcript of *Newsnight*, 6 February 2003

Then there was Frank, the black helicopter –
except he wasn't really a black helicopter,
    they never are. He grew up
in The Just-World Hypothesis
which says that people to whom bad
things happen deserve them and good things
    happen to you because you're good.
When something bad happens to *you*
we call it accident.

On Sundays they took him to the Peak District
to practice levitation. All these bi-polar dreams,
    he remarked, of the Correspondence
Theory of Truth. He stood before the Angel of the North,
catapult behind his back. His mother combed, as far
as possible, his hair over his sticking-out ears.
    Gaps showed – in cover-ups of police shootings,

lies told about a war, the deaths
a Prime Minister was responsible for

explaining ('Look . . .') he was unaware
that people *had* been flying, all this time –
    flying from our peaks and our troughs
into puddled cement bunkers
speckled with handcuffs and water-boards
in Egypt, Morocco, Afghanistan. In his GCSE
    Use of English exam, Frank wrote, 'Man
is the only animal that can imagine pain.'
And then – *Das Lied von der Erde.*

Capoeira Boy

I saw him on YouTube. He was learning the martial art
that masks fighting as dance; the rocking, foot-
to-foot *ginga* bracing him for kicks, swipes
and thistle-light acrobalance. He was finding how to spin,

feint, soar with his opponent. You could worry about him,
at least I did, but I saw he was loved. A favourite
perhaps. Enough anyway to give hope a chance
despite his lumbering, faintly victim, stance

as the two circled each other, holding their arms
off their torsos like cormorants drying their wings.
He was seven or eight, wearing glasses. Eagerness
shone out of him inside the ring of boys

chanting to a tambourine. They knew slaves in Brazil
made the rules. *Only by dance do you learn how to fight.*
Only by fight how to dance. And also that kids like them,
on the West Bank, could learn this in Hebron.

I saw him on YouTube in Jalazoun Refugee Camp.
The teacher, laughing, supervised falls, accidents,
cat's whisker escapes. I imagined he was telling them
Squat and spin! Flat on your hands! Aim your kick in his face –

let him duck – then cartwheel away. This is all about you
but you're nothing without him. Let the dance-fight-dance
set you free. Free of the six-lane motorway
shaking the camp with its sorrowful vibrations.

Free of the twenty-foot wall of cement, a stage set for *Macbeth*.
Grey olives flickered beyond, on hills where I guessed
older men like his grandfather were born
and are forbidden to graze sheep or tend their trees again.

While the boys danced, I pictured the flame of a split aorta
in the chest of a man who has lived all his days in the camps
and will die in one now. Afternoon flowed
through rows of tents like mist coming off black jade

as each became the other's mirror. They were twin lights
in a sconce, tiger cubs perfecting life skills – pounce timing,
split speed for the *roda* – each pouring all he was
into the little space between self's flying heel and other's face.

Pieter the Funny One

Paint us, they said, the world as it is. No more
of your children's games and peasant weddings.
He painted *Procession to Calvary*, Saul
blasted by glory on the way to Damascus.

At home, now, transposing Holy Land to his own
familiar yellows, he did *Adoration of the Kings*
in snow. He was good at snow. Go on
they said. He did *Flight into Egypt*,

a *Census at Bethlehem*, branchy veins
down a red hound's legs.
Not one was satisfied. He made smoke
like dry ice lift over a busted chandelier

in debris just that shade of dun
we see night after night on TV
in a totally annihilated village.
There are bodies in there you can't see,

he said. Forty disabled kids
with their mothers. And a Beirut reporter.
That's more like it, they said. We want
the world we live in. He painted *Slaughter*

of the Innocents (putting them too in snow)
and three hundred thousand refugees
in a red and black landscape.
Not hell, but it could have been.

From a plasma screen
he painted a boy of twelve – his mouth
that black bone shape like the howl in the mask
of Tragedy – plastered crimson

head to toe, standing over
his mother's living torso;
her arms taken off by bomb-blast
on the way to Damascus.

He conjured the home of the Caliphs
in flames like orange lilies – thrown
by an emperor whose religion
was founded on mercy –

and a game-show host from Nebraska,
upset the President of Iraq didn't get
that Israel had a right to defend itself.
(By now the boy's mother had died.)

He started a new thing, skeletons
knifing a king,
another side-saddle on a grey horse
in the shafts of a broke-wheeled caboose

laden with bodies; a lone corpse
floating, swelled belly upwards,
downriver, dogs gnawing the face
of a toddler: plus three-headed Cerberus,

one head searching for fleas, one head
asleep, the third keeping watch
on a black bird making its nest
in red jasmine. They praised

the painstaking draughtsmanship
in his torn men dying on wheels,
failed rebels stuck on poles
in cassis-coloured sky

and black plumes on a high thin horizon
from cities on fire: including
I may say Nazareth. And Bethlehem
where the emperor's pin-up,

a.k.a. the Prince of Peace, was born.
He said that's what I've seen. Yes,
they said, that's what we wanted.
The Triumph of Death.

Birds on the Western Front

Your mess-tin cover's lost. Kestrels hover
above the shelling. They don't turn a feather
when their hunting ground explodes

in a rain of yellow earth
and flares from the Revelation of St John.
You look away, from the artillery

lobbing roar and suck and snap
against one corner of a thicket,
to the partridge of the war zone

making its nest in shattered clods.
As history floods into subsoil
to be blown apart, you cling

to the hard dry stars of observation.
It's how you survive. They were all at it then:
Orchids of the Crimea,

nature notes from the trench
leaving everything unsaid – hell's cauldron
with souls pushed in

and demons stoking flames beneath –
for the pink-flecked wings of a chaffinch
lead-flashed like medieval glass.

You replace gangrene and gas mask
with dreams of alchemy:
language of the birds

translating human earth
to the abstract and divine.
While tanks and machine-guns

strafed that stricken wood
you watched the chaffinch flutter to and fro
through splintered branches, never a green bough left.

Hundreds lay there wounded. If any, you said,
spotted one small bird
they may have wondered why a thing with wings

would stay in such a place. She must, sure,
have had chicks she was too terrified to feed,
too loyal to desert. Like roots clutching at air

you stick to the lark in early dawn
singing fit to burst but coming over insincere
above plough-land latticed like folds of brain

with shell-ravines where nothing stirs
but rats, jittery sentries and the lice
sliding across your faces every night.

Where every elixir is wrong
you hold to what you know.
A little nature study. A solitary magpie,

blue, blue-black and white, spearing a stand
of willow. One for sorrow. One for Babylon,
Nineveh and Northern France,

for mice and desolation, the burgeoning
barn owl population
and never a green bough left.

Mill Wheel at Bantry

i.m. J. G. Farrell

This twelve-foot torque is the iron ghost
of an ancient wheel turning riveted slats
back and up. Now stuck, now moving again
scattering diamonds from a twisting stream
by the library, bucketing over slimed rock
and combing the tangled grasses' emerald hair.
This gash at the top of town, with its whiff
of Hades, is where we catch our glimpse
of what's below. From here on down
we join the hectic flow to the ordinary:
tarmac, Spar, chip-shops; the dockside cafés
and whispering silver-and-isinglass mud
of Bantry Bay. But churning or still

fortune's wheel sets the pace. This wet rock
grey as a seal diving into the dark,
this pour-down of spark-froth entering town
by way of the burying ground, runs under it all:
under Vickery's, the famine graves,
the boarded-up House of Elegance, the fire station
and two-room museum with memorabilia
of martyrs and butter-making, photos of where we are
as it used to be, reports of sea-wrecks
and sea-rescue, the resin replica
of a cross descrying the quest of St Brendan
for Isles of the Blest. There's been so much
I haven't attended to. So much I didn't see.

To Speak of Distance

To speak of distance and the sanctuary lamp,
something you have to do or find
and a darkness to escape. Never mind
rumours of an immigration gate. Revamp
the passport. Speak of hope, that anchor bird
born on the site of loss, with a thousand
resistance strategies frosting her wings
like mica charms or ancient pilgrim songs
embossed in the Book of Psalms. The task
is to assimilate, to move between the languages –
in your case Arabic, Hebrew, Aramaic, Greek –

and map your journey to the shrine.
Every crossing is a pilgrimage. The hard thing
is to pass; harder still to fold those wings
and drop the mask. Just do it. Translate old words
into new. Through cliffs of fall
and fields of black basaltic lava, take
fresh bearings for the crossing-place.
This is the exodus. Here are the moon and sun
appearing upside down or double. Here are stars
in satellite positions never seen before
struggling for their music to be heard.

On the Art of Kintsugi

Just as the Chinese master
in kilns of Longquan

dropped a Qingbai bowl that took years
to make, trying for the perfect lustre –

shadow-green patina, faint turquoise wash
over wafer-thin kaolin

with an uneven rose glow at the edge
inviting the onlooker to contemplate;

just as he picked shards
off the stone floor

and soldered the crazed
apparently irrevocable breaks

with zig zags of lacquer, resin
and powdered gold

and then what do you know
it was valued in the markets of Jingdezhen

beyond the price of Buddha's Hand Citron
and Emperor's Glaze

worth more, so much more
for the brokenness, so –

but no, wait, it's not what you're thinking,
that I smashed what I had, true

feather-ware translucence,
to smithereens for the sake

of upping the price or even the wonder.
It was accident, slippage through fingers

that wrecked
my once-in-a-blue-moon

celadon. But after the shock
came the joy

of finding and then bringing back
to the world (this is porcelain

we're talking of here, not a life)
what was, or what could have been, lost.

Facing East

This steel shell memorial to two lives,
a composer and his singer, looms at me
before sun-up like a guardian of the earth –
or a freezing North Sea re-run of the birth
of Aphrodite. *Dark*, says the sculptor
in her book. *Dark like a wave born*
backwards, shattering as it breaks.
Light and dark like life and death,
part shining and part rust, with movement
between colours as between the forms.
I creep in and run my hand along a frilled
bronze rim. A bivalve – two shells or
a single broken one, self-joining at the core.
I think of the philandering sigh of ocean,
life-long partners betraying and forgiving
and Plato's cave: the fire, the sun

and how, arguing against his gift, he banned
artists for reflecting our world back
with a false beauty, making real unreal,
enticing us to take the shadow for the thing.
I gaze out, invisible as Echo,
at a lead gauze sea. Over my head
the breaker's cusp is a fanned-card silhouette.
Round the edge, letters punched out of metal
like finger-holes in a flute, write in paling sky,
I hear the voices of the drowned. Iron cloud
on the horizon splices day from night
like west from east. On the news
is flat-to-flat urban warfare in Aleppo

and air attacks on Gaza. Over here, in kitchens,
at the Tuesday evening pub quiz, on the bus or tube,
how quickly arguments flare up

even in England; even if we've never been
to what we call the middle of the east.
We identify. Some chasm through the centre
must be in and of us all: creatures of relation
and division, always wrong-footed by the past
on its bed of ice, the sub-tectonic clash
of ancient histories on common ground.
Suddenly I see this rifted arabesque,
a monument to music joined only at its core,
is all of us. *Harmonia*'s gift is cursed.
She can't help it, she's Aphrodite's child –
one false note and what you get is discord –
and her father, lord of war,
is Apollo's enemy. East or west, the first thing
looting soldiers smash (before starting on God's
perfect instrument, the larynx) is an oud or violin.

Sing the sadness and pain of *Sabah*,
the microtonal range of the *maqam*.
Hijaz, conjuring distant desert
and our longing for it. Sing the body:
tongue and teeth to whistle through,
palms to clap, lips to hum, vibrate
or tremble, and the fragile, mucus-laden
vox humana. Sing also of David's harp
placed sideways on the mountain, pitched

to catch wind blowing from rocks
below the tower of Lebanon which looks
toward the oldest city in the world –
whose sky burns indigo, dark-pearled
as strong espresso, above the fountain
in Umayyad Mosque. Where children
used to lick orchid-root ice cream

from *Bakdash Parlour* and now play
Asking-for-Papers-of-Identity-
at-Gun-Point. Where Saladin
and the head of John the Baptist
both lie buried. Where old men
with pewter urns poured tamarisk-
flavour liquorice in sudden jumps,
the way a flat stone skims water.
Al Fayha, Fragrant City, home
to *rosa damascena* and the damask plum:
these dawn-lit pebbles of the west
glow like your hieroglyph intarsia
whose weavers set compound floats
of warp and weft at angles to reflect
light scatter-wise, depending who you are
and where you're looking from.

What will survive are meanings we have found
in what the world has made. Like the calm
rufous freckling of those burnished steps –
infused with cardamom, I remember –
to Al-Hamidiyah Souq beside the citadel.

And at the top, strings of hanging flip-flops,
rosewood sets of backgammon like puzzle books
inlaid with mother-of-pearl, glinting gargoyle fish
and stalls of uncut samite, whose glitter-twill
depends on optic interference like the play of light
in Damascus Twist, the iron-plait steel
of sword blades and gun-barrels:
the mystery metal welded in carbon fire
which can cut a rifle muzzle or a hair
floating across a dagger. Whose laminate spirals,
acid-bitten into waves, resemble damask.

What would we be without desire for form?
Pattern keeps us safe. We look for omens in a flock
of redwing, the gods' will in dappled entrails,
the outline of a story in the stars. We break the line
to shape it, string catgut over membrane,
set up a ten-foot memorial
to music – a scallop shell, a pilgrim's prayer –
in shale of an eroding coast
and turn it east to face the storm.
Voices of the drowned. I watch dawn
gild the sea to iridescence. Sea-birds arc
and squawk and flicker-print the air.
Breakers roar on draining shingle.
Palmetto patterns dint the waves
from grey to silver, hyacinth and jade.
Making is our defence against the dark.

Chain made from a broom handle.

Reprinted with kind permission from the Archives of Yad Vashem
& World Center for Holocaust Research, Documentation,
Education and Commemoration

Notes

'The Electrification of Beth Shalom' – Crete's Jewish community, dating from the third century BC before the first destruction of the Temple, was one of the oldest in the world. In 1911, Crete's last Arch Rabbi was photographed standing beside the new-lit lamps of the great medieval synagogue Beth Shalom, the first building in Hania to have electric light. In 1941, eight years after he died, that synagogue was destroyed by German bombs. In 1944, all Cretan Jews were arrested and put on a boat, which was torpedoed and sunk twelve hours later.

'The Chain' – Yad Vashem's Holocaust History Museum contains a wooden broom-handle carved into a chain with scenes of camp life incised on the links. It was made in a French-run Nazi detention camp by Moshe ('Max') Scheiner, a Polish Jew living in France. He was arrested in 1941, gave the chain to his wife and in 1942 was deported to Auschwitz-Birkenau, where he died. His brother Armand Szainer donated it to the collection.

'After the Fire' – Hania's smaller synagogue Etz Hayyim was plundered by the Nazis in 1944 and left derelict. Restored in 1996, it is now a practising synagogue open to all faiths, a memorial and archive for the lost community. In 2012 it was attacked twice by arsonists.

'A Guide to the Church of Nativity in Time of Siege' – On Easter Tuesday 2002, Israel Defence Forces invaded Bethlehem searching for Palestinian militants. For thirty-nine days, citizens as well as two hundred monks were besieged in the Church of the Nativity.

'Seven Words and an Earthquake' – The Seven Last Words or Sayings of Christ from the Cross form part of services and meditations in Holy Week. Excerpted from the Gospels, they move from displacing pain onto other people to admitting feelings of abandonment and need, and finally fulfilment and reunion. Josef Haydn was commissioned to write music to play between a bishop's Easter reflections on these Sayings in Cádiz Cathedral in 1787.

Following Matthew's account of what happened after Christ died ('The earth did quake and the rocks rent') Haydn added an aftermath, *Il Terremoto*. He must have been thinking partly of the Lisbon Earthquake, which struck on All

Saints' Day 1755 and destroyed Lisbon's churches, devastated Spanish cities including Cádiz and caused floods from North Africa to Cornwall as well as tremors in faith throughout Enlightenment Europe. Down the centuries, pathologists and physicians have put forward many different detailed explanations of the precise cause of death in crucifixion.

'As I Flick the Remote in the Gulf I Think of an Ancient Greek Playwright' – The first stanza is my translation of Euripides' *Trojan Women*, lines 379–84. This play was first put on in 415 BC, the year after Athens destroyed its ally Melos. When the Melians refused to pay tribute and seceded from alliance, Athens sacked the town, killed the men and enslaved the women. The play is often seen as Euripides' criticism of a foreign policy which illicitly transformed alliance into empire. Gilbert Murray's 1905 translation made it a critique of British imperialism; later versions have evoked political scenarios from nuclear war to post-9/11 America.

'The Just-World Hypothesis' – In social psychology, the Just-World Hypothesis is the assumption that the results of human acts are morally fair: good acts are rewarded, bad ones punished. In the philosophical concept of a 'correspondence' theory of truth, the truth of a statement is determined by how it relates to the world, how accurately it describes reality. It is now accepted that information about Saddam Hussein's weapons, which Tony Blair gave the British Parliament in March 2003, on the basis of which Parliament voted to join the United States' invasion of Iraq, was not true.
Black Helicopter: Conspiracy theorists in US militia groups believe black helicopters are used as secret agents by the New World Order (the UN, preparing to take over America) or US government, for nefarious purposes like enforcing the Endangered Species Act, preventing ranchers from killing protected wild animals. Some also believe black helicopters are life-forms created to spy on anti-liberals.

'Capoeira Boy' – African slaves on Brazilian plantations, allowed to dance but not fight or bear arms, created a martial art disguised as dance called capoeira, now popular in the west. Volunteers from the charity Bidna Capoeira teach it in refugee camps in the West Bank and East Jerusalem. They find it increases co-operation and a sense of self-worth among children traumatised by violence. *Hebron*: a city in the Judaean mountains in occupied Palestine on the southern West Bank. In 2011, Khelly Hill outside it was declared State Land. Settlers built homes and a road; Palestinian shepherds were denied entry to their land for grazing or cutting grass.

'Pieter the Funny One' – During the Netherlands' revolt against Spain which culminated in the Eighty Years' War, Peter Bruegel the Elder (called 'Pieter the Droll' because he painted children's games and peasant life) created some of the earliest images of social protest in the history of art. He painted *The Triumph of Death* in 1562; I saw it in Madrid in 2006 during Israel's invasion of Lebanon.

'Birds on the Western Front' – Title of an essay by Hector Hugh Munro, whose pen name was Saki, describing bird behaviour over trenches in the First World War. Officially over-age, he refused a commission in 1914, joined up as a trooper and was killed in 1916. The essay was published posthumously in 1924.

'On the Art of Kintsugi' – The Japanese art of Kintsugi – mending a broken pot with golden seams which render it more valuable than before – makes a virtue of accidental destruction. It is considered dishonourable to smash the pot deliberately.

'Facing East' – *Dark like the belly of a wave . . . between the forms*: from Maggi Hambling's book about making her monument to Benjamin Britten (with Peter Pears in mind), *The Aldeburgh Scallop* (Full Circle Press, Suffolk, 2010).
Harmonia: Harmonia was child of an illicit union between sex and violence. Her mother was Aphrodite, goddess of love, her father was Ares, god of war. Aphrodite's jealous husband Hephaestus gave Harmonia as a wedding gift a necklace which brought disaster to its owner. Harmonia was eventually transformed into a snake; her daughter Semele inherited the necklace, so did her descendant Jocasta and Jocasta's son Polynices. All came to grief in spectacular tragedies. To stop it doing more harm, the necklace was dedicated at Delphi, in the precinct of Apollo, god of music.
Damascus Twist: No one knows exactly how Damascus steel was made. Recent research has revealed within it nanowires and carbon nanotubes of an extraordinary length-to-width ratio.

Acknowledgements

Many thanks to Nikos Stavroulakis for sharing his learning and insight into Crete's Jewish and Muslim past, and for an invitation to teach poetry in Etz Hayyim Synagogue. Also to Graham and Peggy Reid, who heard Le Trio Joubran, Palestinian brothers from four generations of oud-makers and players, in Macedonia and introduced me to them in London.

Thanks also to Tring Chamber Music for a commission to write poems between movements of Haydn's *Seven Last Words;* to Paul Barritt, Catherine Yates, Robin Ireland and Josephine Horder for inspiring performances in Ashridge Chapel at Easter 2013; and to David Waterman for illuminating discussions of Haydn's music. Thanks to Situations for *Nowhereisland,* a project by artist Alex Hartley for the London 2012 Cultural Olympiad, for commissioning 'To Speak of Distance'; to Carol Ann Duffy for commissioning a poem for an anthology commemorating the First World War; to Rupert and Elizabeth Nabarro for their flat in Hania where some of these poems were written; and to Alexander Phoundoulakis of Etz Hayyim for telling me about *kintsugi.*

Thanks to my 2011 poetry workshop at West Cork Literary Festival and librarians at Bantry Library; to Etz Hayyim Synagogue, especially librarian Anja Zückmantel and my 2012 poetry workshop there; and Yad Vashem, World Center for Holocaust Research, Documentation, Education and Commemoration, for sending an image to refresh my memory of Moshe Scheiner's chain.

Thanks also to editors and publishers of the following publications where some of these poems first appeared: *1914: Poetry Remembers* (Faber, 2013), *Aeon, Arvon Poetry Competition Winners 2007, Asymptote, The Caravan, The Critical Muslim, Interlitq, The*

Liberal, London Review of Books, The New Humanist, New Welsh Review, The New Yorker, Night & Day, Plume, Poem, Poetry Ireland Review, Poetry London, Poetry Review, The Poet's Quest for God: 21st Century Poems of Faith, Doubt and Wonder (eds Dr O. Brennan, T. Swift and D. Bury, Eyewear Publishing 2014), *Rialto, Standpoint, The Stinging Fly* and www.nowhereisland.org. Thanks also to the digital publication produced for the sixth edition of the Abraaj Group Art Prize 2014, www.gardenandspring.com which presented some of these poems alongside work by artist Abbas Akhavan, *Study for a Hanging Garden*. 'Landscape with Flight into Egypt' and 'Pieter the Funny One' were published in *The Mara Crossing* (Chatto & Windus, 2012).

Many thanks to my editor Parisa Ebrahimi for her painstaking work and eagle eye, and also to Phillip Birch, Gwen Burnyeat, Ian Duhig, Eva Hoffman and Aamer Hussein.